ROCKY MOUNTAIN WILDLIFE

Nature Activity Book

James Kavanagh
Illustrations By Raymond Leung

To order, call 800-434-2555; Fax: 602-681-3343
To share comments, email us at editor@waterfordpress.com
For information on custom-published products, call 800-434-2555.
ISBN: 978-158355-583-5

Word Search

Find the names of these Rocky Mountain mammals.

Q O Y G C L A A G D E H W Z M N
V A Z W D X M B B V H S L Q H J
O D R B S A S M L F J O X T I N
M M M M R Y K Z A K M F G H N R
B F C J U F U X C R E Z H E O E
H L I V M S N Q K F M P G G J D
F X B L W Y K L B J P O I P Q S
Y J K E N A X R E D I R T A P Q
C G D A A P M I A Z K C S N B U
L J R V J V M L R T A U V E P I
S Y E J F Q E C U H M P M D O R
S T E O Z Q D R X V I I H N L R
S N D T B B O J Q R X N N D S E
F B I K H K P S H H S E X C M L
C G C L M S U H X C E W P W C I
R B L W I J H L Q G J D X D P R

PORCUPINE

PIKA

RED SQUIRREL

MARMOT

SKUNK

MUSKRAT

BLACK BEAR

BEAVER

Answers

Name Match

Draw a line between the animal and its name.

1.

SARA ORANGETIP

BLACK-CAPPED CHICKADEE

CUTTHROAT TROUT

MOUNTAIN BLUEBIRD

FLYING SQUIRREL

MOUNTAIN GOAT

GREAT HORNED OWL

COUGAR

2.

3.

4.

5.

6.

7.

8.

Color Me

Western Tanager

color key

Anise Swallowtail

color key

Spot the Differences

Try to spot 10 differences between the images.

Answers

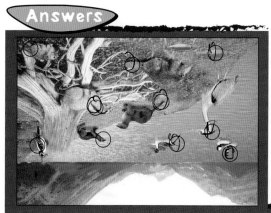

Home Sweet Home

There are a number of habitats in the Rockies that support a unique community of animals that feed and live there.

Draw a line between the animal and its habitat.
(Note: Many animals can live in several habitats)

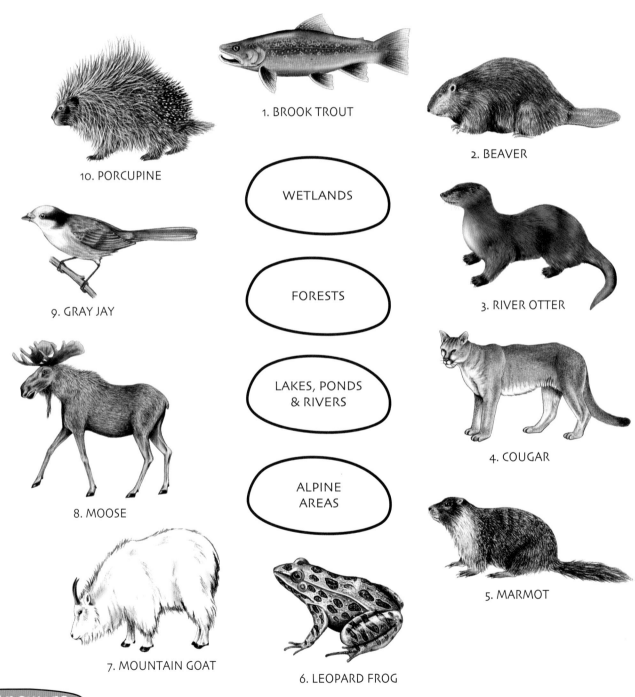

1. BROOK TROUT

2. BEAVER

10. PORCUPINE

WETLANDS

FORESTS

LAKES, PONDS & RIVERS

ALPINE AREAS

9. GRAY JAY

3. RIVER OTTER

4. COUGAR

8. MOOSE

5. MARMOT

7. MOUNTAIN GOAT

6. LEOPARD FROG

Make Words

The **Yellow-bellied Marmot** is a large rodent that lives in alpine areas of the Rockies. A social animal, it lives in groups of up to several dozen individuals. When the colony forages in meadows for food, one or two individuals stand guard over the troop. If danger approaches, the guards will whistle loudly causing the group to retreat underground to the safety of their burrows.

How many words can you make from the letters in its name?

_____   _____

_____   _____

_____   _____

_____   _____

_____   _____

_____   _____

_____   _____

_____   _____

Answers

Possible answers include: Arm, arty, beam, beard, beat, beet, belie, bell, bellow, belly, belt, blame, blow, dart, debtor, delete, dell, dial, dime, dirt, dolly, lamb, lame, lie, lime, low, lowly, malt, mellow, melt, mold, mole, my, rally, ram, rye, tame, toiled, tomb, wail, walled, way, welder, worm, wry, yell

Origami

Starting with a square piece of paper, follow the folding instructions below to create a bat.

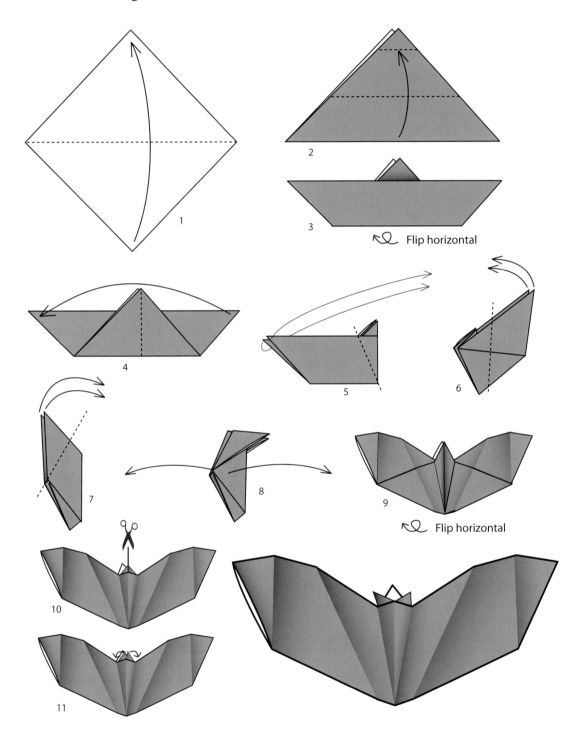

Flip horizontal

Flip horizontal

Be An Artist

Draw this bird by copying it one square at a time.

The **Common Raven** is a large black bird found throughout the Rocky Mountain region. It is distinguished from the similar American crow by its large size, its large, broad beak and its call which is a horse croak as opposed to a distinct – *caw*. Ravens are among the most intelligent bird species and are capable of remarkable feats of problem-solving. They are revered for their intelligence and spirit by many cultures.

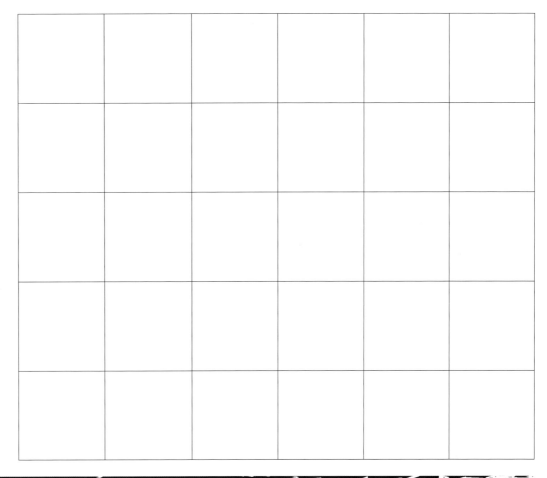

Word Search

Find the names of these Rocky Mountain birds.

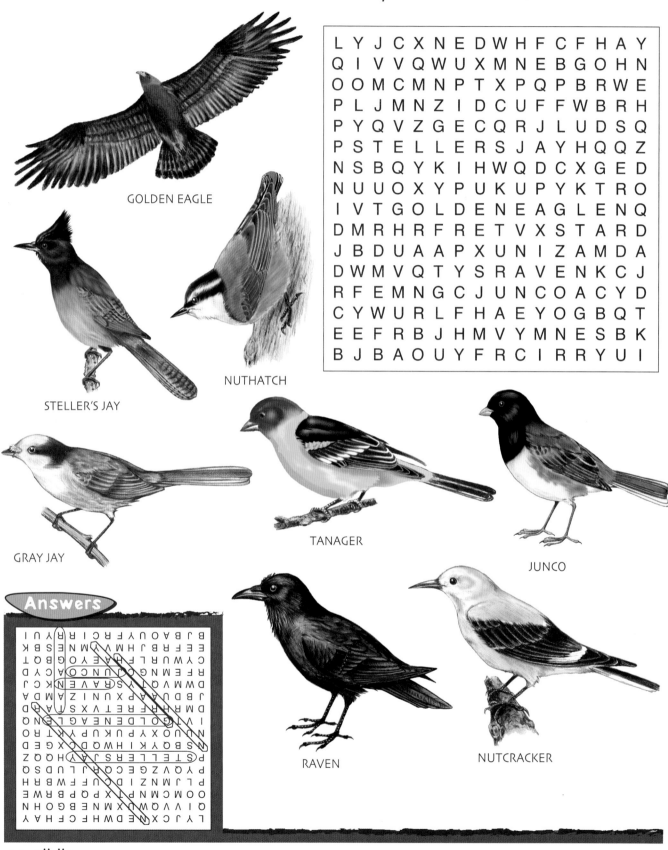

GOLDEN EAGLE

NUTHATCH

STELLER'S JAY

GRAY JAY

TANAGER

JUNCO

RAVEN

NUTCRACKER

```
L Y J C X N E D W H F C F H A Y
Q I V V Q W U X M N E B G O H N
O O M C M N P T X P Q P B R W E
P L J M N Z I D C U F F W B R H
P Y Q V Z G E C Q R J L U D S Q
P S T E L L E R S J A Y H Q Q Z
N S B Q Y K I H W Q D C X G E D
N U U O X Y P U K U P Y K T R O
I V T G O L D E N E A G L E N Q
D M R H R F R E T V X S T A R D
J B D U A A P X U N I Z A M D A
D W M V Q T Y S R A V E N K C J
R F E M N G C J U N C O A C Y D
C Y W U R L F H A E Y O G B Q T
E E F R B J H M V Y M N E S B K
B J B A O U Y F R C I R R Y U I
```

Answers

Name Scramble

Unscramble the letters to form the names of these animals.

1.

A	E	E	L	G

2.

R	G	I	Z	L	Y	Z

3.

K	E	W	P	E	C	O	R	O	D

4.

F	T	U	T	E	R	B	L	Y

5.

E	R	A	B	V	E

6.

R	E	S	U	R	L	I	Q

7.

C	U	I	P	N	K	M	H

8.

C	D	K	U

Connect The Dots

Connect the dots in numeric order to reveal a mammal that feeds on salmon it catches in mountain streams.

Who am I?

The **Striped Skunk** is one of the most common and widespread North American mammals. They are often smelled before they are seen since they exude an unpleasant odor. When threated, they spray aggressors with a foul liquid that is so unpleasant, many predators like foxes, wolves and cougars do not hunt them. A true omnivore, it eats a wide variety of plants and animals.

Help the skunk find something to eat

ENTER

Animal Tracks

Match the mammal to its track.

CHIPMUNK

I have light tracks with 4 toes on my front feet and 5 toes on my back feet.

1.

2.

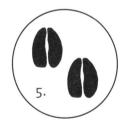
3.

4.

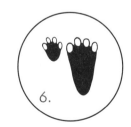
5.

6.

COUGAR

My tracks have rounded toes and my claws don't show because they are retracted when I walk.

BEAVER

My tracks are unusual because in soft mud you can see the webbing between my toes.

ELK

Like most hoofed animals, my tracks have two long toes that make up my track.

GRAY WOLF

I have tracks like a pet dog, with 4 toes on each foot and my claws always show.

SNOWSHOE HARE

I have long back feet and short front feet. All my feet have four toes. I am named for my large back feet that help me move through deep snow.

Who Am I?

Name these animals.

1. I am a small bird named for my color and my beautiful singing voice.

_____

4. I'm a common bird of prey named for the color of my tail.

_____

2. My coat of barbed quills helps protect me from predators.

_____

5. I'm a hoofed mammal named for my white tail which is held upright when I run.

_____

3. I'm a popular sport fish named for the colorful stripe down my side.

_____

6. I'm a clever mammal named for the color of my fur.

_____

Oddball Out

In each row, circle the animal which is different from the others.

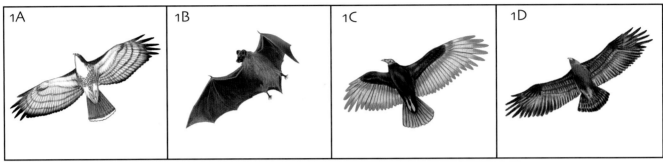

Three of these are birds, one is not.

Three of these are squirrels, one is not.

Three of these ducks, one is not.

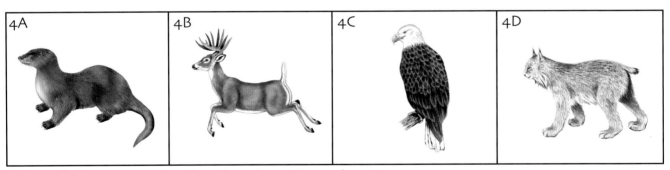

Three of these are meat-eaters (carnivores), one is not.

Word Search

Find the names of these Rocky Mountain predators.

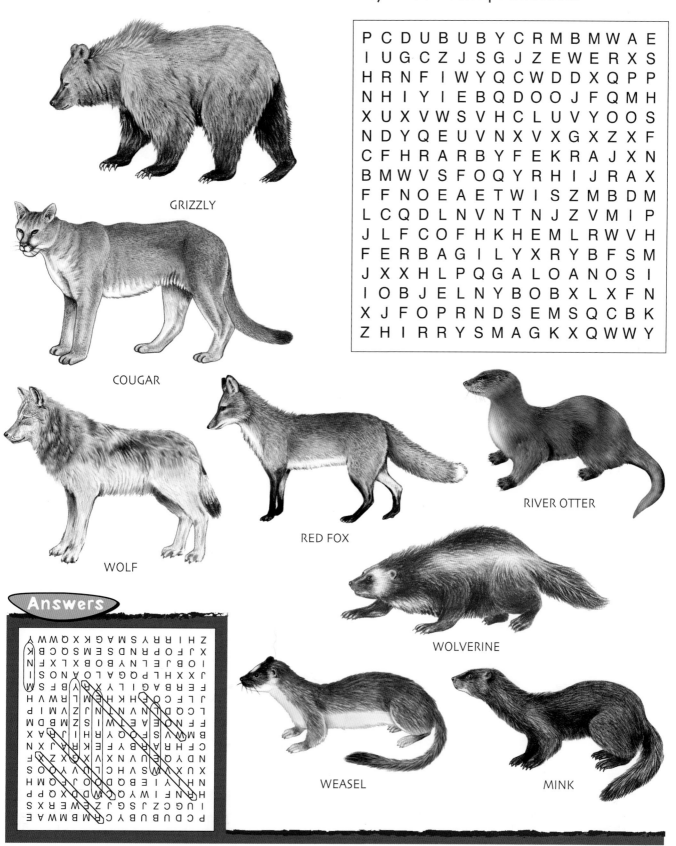

P C D U B U B Y C R M B M W A E
I U G C Z J S G J Z E W E R X S
H R N F I W Y Q C W D D X Q P P
N H I Y I E B Q D O O J F Q M H
X U X V W S V H C L U V Y O O S
N D Y Q E U V N X V X G X Z X F
C F H R A R B Y F E K R A J X N
B M W V S F O Q Y R H I J R A X
F F N O E A E T W I S Z M B D M
L C Q D L N V N T N J Z V M I P
J L F C O F H K H E M L R W V H
F E R B A G I L Y X R Y B F S M
J X X H L P Q G A L O A N O S I
I O B J E L N Y B O B X L X F N
X J F O P R N D S E M S Q C B K
Z H I R R Y S M A G K X Q W W Y

GRIZZLY

COUGAR

WOLF

RED FOX

RIVER OTTER

WOLVERINE

WEASEL

MINK

Answers

17

Name Match

Draw a line between the colorful animal and its name.

1.

WHITE-TAILED
DEER

5.

RED-TAILED
HAWK

2.

GRAY WOLF

6.

RUFOUS
HUMMINGBIRD

BLACK
BEAR

7.

3.

RED-WINGED
BLACKBIRD

4.

ORANGE
SULPHUR

8.

YELLOW
WARBLER

Shadow Know-How

Can you identify these Rocky Mountain animals?

1. Bat   2. Woodpecker   3. Mountain goat   4. Trout   5. Grizzly   6. Deer   7. Fox   8. Skunk

Be An Artist

Draw this mammal by copying it one square at a time.

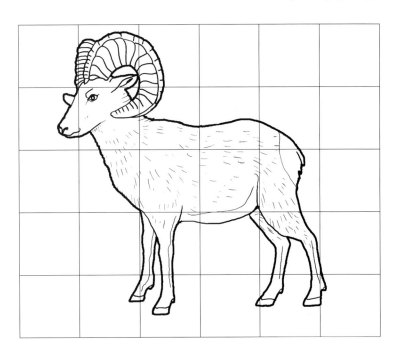

The **Bighorn Sheep** is distinguished by its huge curling horns. It lives in high mountain areas and has special hooves adapted to stick to rocks like suction cups. During breeding season the males compete for females by rushing at each other and smashing their horns into each other. For this reason, males have specially adapted skulls so they don't get injured by head-smashing.

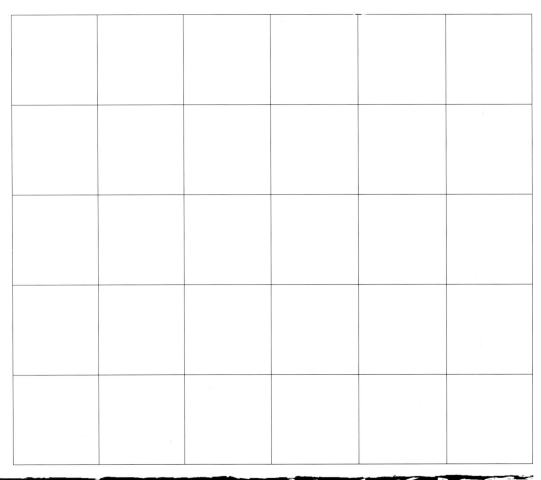

You Are What You Eat

Herbivores eat mostly plants. Carnivores eat other animals.
Omnivores eat plants and animals.

Draw a line between the animal and its diet.

WOOD DUCK

WOLF

OMNIVORE

MOOSE

PORCUPINE

HERBIVORE

RACCOON

CARNIVORE

STRIPED SKUNK

LYNX

MINK

Make Words

The **Black Bear** – is common throughout the Rocky Mountains. Its coat color is usually black, but in the northern Rockies cinnamon and brown bears are also common. A true omnivore, it feeds on a variety of plants and animals but its diet is estimated to be 85% vegetarian. Black bears are easily distinguished from their more dangerous cousin, the grizzly, by their snout which is straight in profile. Grizzlies have a more concave or "dished" face.

How many words can you make from the letters in its name?

_____   _____

_____   _____

_____   _____

_____   _____

_____   _____

_____   _____

_____   _____

Answers

Possible answers include: be, bar, bra, ale, are, car, real, bear, race, lace, bale, kale, lack, back, rack, black, blare, clear

Word Search

Find the names of these Rocky Mountain fishes.

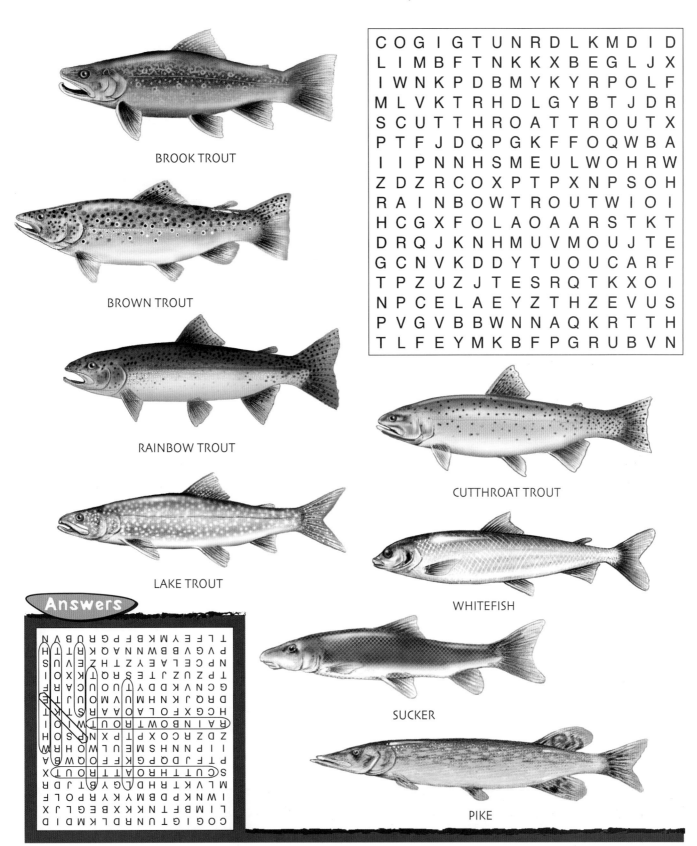

BROOK TROUT

BROWN TROUT

RAINBOW TROUT

LAKE TROUT

CUTTHROAT TROUT

WHITEFISH

SUCKER

PIKE

C O G I G T U N R D L K M D I D
L I M B F T N K K X B E G L J X
I W N K P D B M Y K Y R P O L F
M L V K T R H D L G Y B T J D R
S C U T T H R O A T T R O U T X
P T F J D Q P G K F F O Q W B A
I I P N N H S M E U L W O H R W
Z D Z R C O X P T P X N P S O H
R A I N B O W T R O U T W I O I
H C G X F O L A O A A R S T K T
D R Q J K N H M U V M O U J T E
G C N V K D D Y T U O U C A R F
T P Z U Z J T E S R Q T K X O I
N P C E L A E Y Z T H Z E V U S
P V G V B B W N N A Q K R T T H
T L F E Y M K B F P G R U B V N

Answers

Class Act

There are five classes of vertebrates (animals with backbones) that live in the Rocky Mountains.

Draw a line between the animal and the class it belongs to.

1. WESTERN TANAGER

2. LITTLE BROWN BAT

10. BIGHORN SHEEP

MAMMAL

BIRD

3. BROOK TROUT

9. TIGER SALAMANDER

REPTILE

AMPHIBIAN

4. CHORUS FROG

8. JUNCO

FISH

5. PAINTED TURTLE

7. MUSKRAT

6. GOPHER SNAKE

Origami

Starting with a square piece of paper, follow the folding instructions below to create a rabbit.

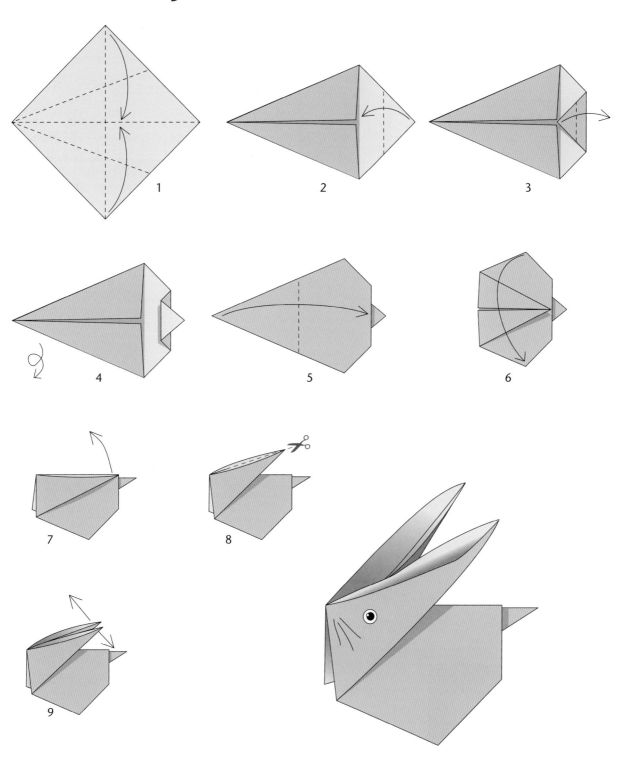

Crossword

Across

2. Another name for a cougar (2 words).

....

4. "Crazy like a _ _ _."

....

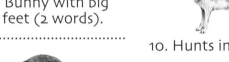

6. Bunny with big feet (2 words).

....

7. Dam builder.

9. Makes "bugling" calls during mating season.

....

10. Hunts in packs.

....

11. _ _ _ _ _ _ _ _ _ goat.

Down

1. Named for its large curled horns.

....

2. Deer named for its huge ears (2 words).

....

3. Large weasel.

5. Biggest bear in the Rockies.

....

8. Also known as reindeer.

Food Chain

Draw a line between the species and its place in the food chain.

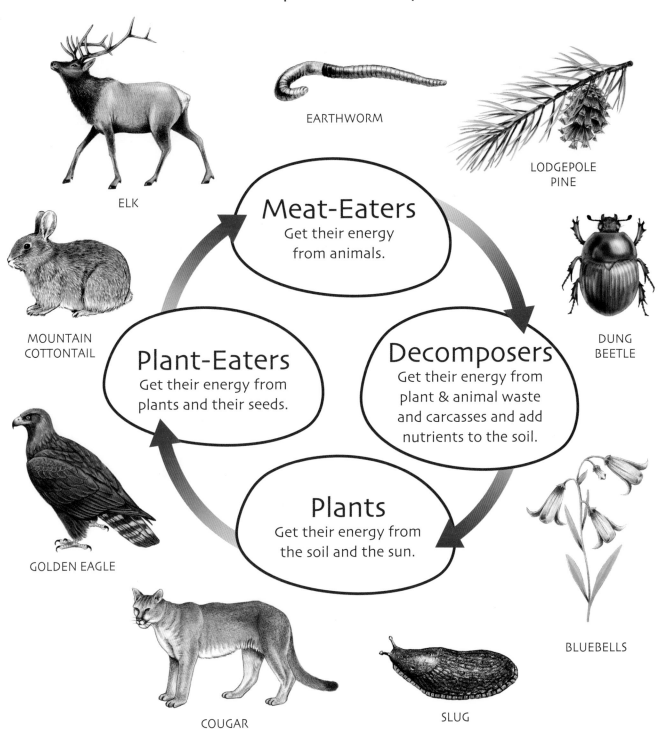

ELK

EARTHWORM

LODGEPOLE PINE

MOUNTAIN COTTONTAIL

Meat-Eaters
Get their energy from animals.

DUNG BEETLE

Plant-Eaters
Get their energy from plants and their seeds.

Decomposers
Get their energy from plant & animal waste and carcasses and add nutrients to the soil.

GOLDEN EAGLE

Plants
Get their energy from the soil and the sun.

BLUEBELLS

COUGAR

SLUG

Shadow Know-How

Can you identify these horned mammals?

Fold-In

This hoofed animal is one of largest land animals in North America and can weigh up to 1,300 lbs. (600 kg). The males have large antlers which are shed each year. The antlers regrow each summer before the autumn "rut", a ritual competition between males for females. Winning males then begin a loud screaming – called "bugling" – to attract females from miles away. This call is one of the most distinctive sounds of the Rockies.

C→   Fold   ←C   B→   Fold   ←B   A→   Fold   ←A

D | GFO | EL IJS | TU | K | PC | TH
ZY | E | D X | Y | | MS | EA

Connect The Dots

Connect the dots in numeric order to reveal a mammal that is known for its huge size and massive horns.

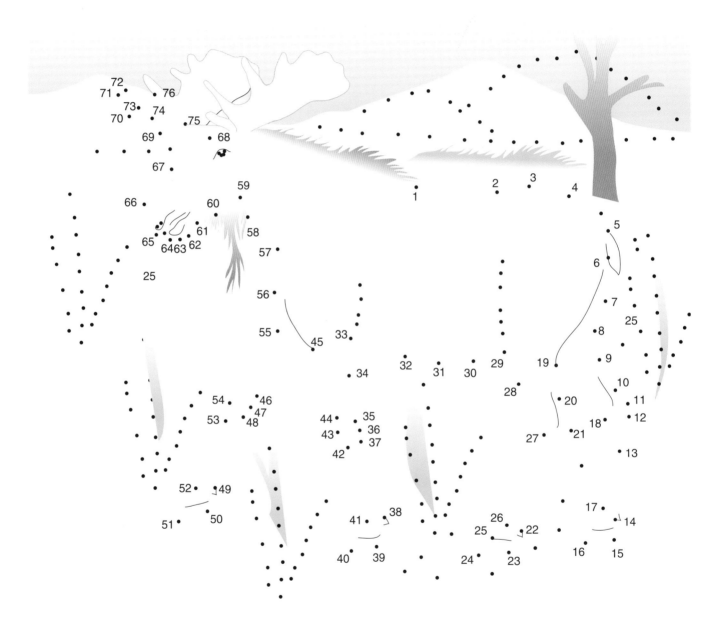

What am I?

Picture Scramble

Place the numbers 1 through 9 in the lettered boxes
on the right to create the image on the left.

BLUE GROUSE

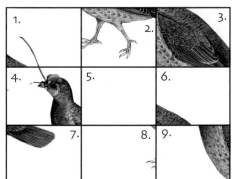

A	B	C
D	E 3	F
G	H	I

BOBCAT

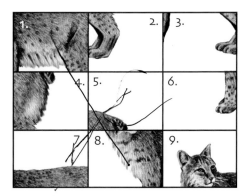

A	B	C
D	E 1	F
G	H	I

RED-NAPED
SAPSUCKER

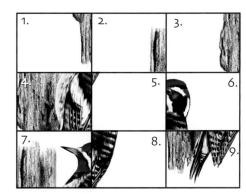

A	B	C
D	E 4	F
G	H	I

Answers

31

Word Search

Find the names of these Rocky Mountain butterflies.

PAINTED LADY

FRITILLARY

```
J Y C B B M W D Q P B M I W G Q
C R U U I T H B D O H Z B J K Y
I U Q K O H O L T Q B B L X Z T
B K I U F C R E S C E N T L I E
O F P H F C A Y G O S G D K L N
G K K A R S N Q Y M W Y T J A X
F V K I I B G S A M A S I F S Y
I G V R T N E H D A L A P H R G
I U U S I N T N V S L J Z Y S M
A K P T L B I E B D O N M U C M
Q W H R L P P I D S W G I Y R P
K Z M E A S I X T L T A I Y P E
D R Q A R V E G Y D A Q V U R F
O D C K Y Q K Y D L I D F U S V
V V W J U U Q C D F L U Y F O A
X Z B G Z X S S E N J X W X Q B
```

SWALLOWTAIL

ORANGETIP

COMMA

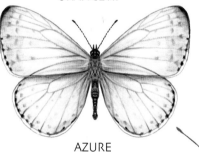

AZURE

HAIRSTREAK

CRESCENT